The Beggar's Opera

Adapted by David Turner
from John Gay's play

Music arranged by
Roy Darby

Samuel French–London
New York – Sydney – Toronto – Hollywood

© 1982 BY DAVID TURNER (book)

This play is fully protected under the copyright laws of the British Commonwealth of Nations, the United States of America, and all countries of the Berne and Universal Copyright Conventions.

All rights are strictly reserved.

It is an infringement of the copyright to give any public performance or reading of this play either in its entirety or in the form of excerpts without the prior consent of the copyright owners. No part of this publication may be transmitted, stored in a retrieval system, or reproduced in any form or by any means, electronic, mechanical, photocopying, manuscript, typescript, recording, or otherwise, without the prior permission of the copyright owners.

SAMUEL FRENCH LTD, 26 SOUTHAMPTON STREET, STRAND, LONDON WC2E 7JE, or their authorized agents, issue licences to amateurs to give performances of this play on payment of a fee. **This fee is subject to contract and subject to variation at the sole discretion of Samuel French Ltd.**

Licences are issued subject to the understanding that it shall be made clear in all advertising matter that the audience will witness an amateur performance; and that the names of the authors of the plays shall be included on all announcements and on all programmes.

The publication of this play must not be taken to imply that it is necessarily available for performance by amateurs or professionals, either in the British Isles or overseas. Amateurs intending production must, in their own interests, make application to Samuel French Ltd or their authorized agents, for consent before starting rehearsals or booking a theatre or hall.

Applications to perform the play by professionals should be made to HARVEY UNNA AND STEPHEN DURBRIDGE LTD, 24 Pottery Lane, Holland Park, London W11 4LZ

ISBN 0 573 08053 4

Please note our NEW ADDRESS:

Samuel French Ltd
52 Fitzroy Street London W1P 6JR
Tel: 01 - 387 9373

CHARACTERS

The Beggar, the author of the piece
Mr Peachum, a notorious fence and informer
Mrs Peachum, his common-law wife
Polly Peachum, their daughter
Filch, their servant and part-time child-getter at
    Newgate
Mr Lockit, chief Jailer of Newgate Prison
Lucy Lockit, his daughter
Captain Macheath, a famous highwayman

Members of Macheath's gang:

Jemmy Twitcher	**Nimming Ned**
Crook-Fingered Jack	**Henry Paddington**
Wat Dreary	**Matt of the Mint**
Robin of Bagshot	**Ben Budge**

Drawer at the Tavern

"Ladies" of the Town:

Mrs Coaxer	**Jenny Diver**
Dolly Trull	**Mrs Slammekin**
Mrs Vixen	**Suky Tawdry**
Betty Doxy	**Molly Brazen**

Two Constables
Servants at Peachum's Warehouse
Mrs Diana Trapes, a brothel keeper
The Judge
Four Women with babies
Jack Ketch, the Hangman
A Messenger

PROLOGUE

Period: 1728

MUSICAL AIRS

PROLOGUE

1	Beggars Now Are Cumen In	Beggar and Company

ACT I

2	Through All The Employments of Life	Peachum and Chorus
3	Virgins Are Like the Fair Flower	Polly
4	Our Polly is a Sad Slut	Mrs Peachum
5	Can Love be Controlled by Advice?	Polly
6	O Polly, You Might Have Toy'd	Mrs Peachum
7	O Ponder Well	Polly
8	The Turtle Thus	Polly
	Through All The Employments of Life (reprise)	Peachum and Mrs Peachum
9	My Heart Forbodes	Polly
10	My Heart Was So Free	Macheath
11	Pretty Polly Say	Polly and Macheath
12	Were I Laid on Greenland's Coast	Macheath and Polly
13	Oh, What Pain It Is To Part	Polly
14	Fill Ev'ry Glass	Highwaymen
15	Let Us Take The Road	Highwaymen
16	If The Heart Of A Man	Macheath
17	Youth's The Season	"Ladies"
18	Before The Barn Door	Jenny
19	At The Tree I Shall Suffer	Macheath
	Youth's The Season (reprise)	"Ladies"
20	Man May Escape	Macheath
21	How Cruel Are The Traitors	Lucy
22	The First Time At The Looking-Glass	Macheath
23	When You Censure The Age	Peachum and Lockit
24	Is Then His Fate Decreed, Sir?	Lucy
25	You'll Think Ere Many Days	Lockit
	When You Censure The Age (reprise)	Peachum and Lockit

ACT II

26	How Happy Could I Be With Either	Macheath
27	I'm Bubbled	Polly and Lucy
28	Cease Your Funning	Polly
29	Why, How Now, Madam Flirt?	Lucy and Polly
30	No Power On Earth	Polly
31	When Young At The Bar	Lucy

The piano/vocal score for this Musical is available on hire from Samuel French Ltd.

PROLOGUE

This short prologue takes place in front of the main setting. Its main aim is to assemble the entire Company by degrees. The performers can enter from the wings or by way of the auditorium. At the director's discretion they can stamp their feet when singing "Yea, Nay"

Beggar

Air 1: Beggars Now Are Cumen In

Beggars now are cumen in,
Loudly sing yea, nay.
Crime is rife and civil strife
Is shortly on its way.
Sing yea, nay.

Law and order's now expected,
Loudly sing yea, nay.
Yours the choice and yours the voice,
So Whigs and Tories say.
Sing yea, nay.

Whores and highwaymen proliferate,
Loudly sing yea, nay,
When need and greed so much do feed
On common disarray.
Sing yea, nay.

Your Royal Majesties, Highnesses, Lords, Ladies, Gentlemen, Squires, Commoners and Riff-Raff . . . I hope I have not left anyone out . . . For I have learned, in this world, that bowing and scraping means everything whilst greeting a fellow creature as man to man means nothing. Allow me, then, to present myself. I am the lowest of the low, a beggar. But I believe the Muses of the gods flow through every man. So I have written a play, an opera. It is a fine, moral tale. The villain of my piece will go to the gallows right and properly, as you would all desire it, and reality would have it. The actors belong to our brotherhood of beggars. The actresses belong to our sisterhood of honest harlots. We're also greenhorn thespians and we revel in it. After all, it makes a change from pilfering and legs-in-the-air. Even the likes of us have a sensibility for the arts, be it known. So without more ado, let me thank the management for their trust in us and present the players.

Peachum and Mrs Peachum join the Beggar on either side

Here come Peachum and his missus,
Loudly sing yea, nay.

They're defrauders and informers
In our roundelay.
Sing yea, nay.

Polly and Macheath enter

Next we meet a pair of lovers,
Loudly sing yea, nay.
Polly's father, Peachum, rather
Loathes their wedding day.
Sing yea, nay.

Her spouse, indeed, is bold Macheath,
Loudly sing yea, nay.
He's a thief and rogue-in-chief
Upon the king's highway.
Sing yea, nay.

Macheath and Polly kiss passionately, shake hands with the Beggar and take their places in the line-up

Lockit and Lucy enter

Lockit is the Newgate jailer,
Loudly sing yea, nay.
Pris'ners he bleeds and grants their needs
If they can money pay.
Sing yea, nay.

Lucy Lockit's Lockit's daughter,
Loudly sing yea, nay,
She's so riggish and so friggish
As tattoo marks display.
Sing yea, nay.

Lockit and Lucy move to join the rest of the assembled cast

My aim is to show you how the lower sorts of people have vices, certainly . . . but only in the same degree as those of the rich. But here come the whores and the highwaymen . . . in fact, the entire company!

The Whores (Women) and Highwaymen enter

All   The rich are always well respected,
Loudly sing yea, nay.
While the poor lie at death's door
Or from the gallows sway.
Sing yea, nay!

To those who have, more shall be given,
Loudly sing yea, nay.
And those who've not in gutters rot,

'Spite what the scriptures say.
Sing yea, nay!

So the whores and highwaymen
Who're gathered here today
With a view to entertain you,
Beg you hear our play!

The music stops and Peachum steps forward

Peachum That's enough, Writer!
Beggar But I was going to explain to the spectators about——
Peachum You've explained sufficiently. What! Would you ruin us by telling them the whole tale before we've started?
Beggar But——
Peachum No buts! Or, as president of our theatrical fraternity, I'll have your name scrubbed from our list at our next monthly meeting. (*To the audience*) Oh, how these writers do give one's buttocks the headache! (*To the Beggar*) Begone! Stand aside, sirrah, and be silent!
Beggar (*tugging at a forelock*) I will, sir, I will . . . Indeed I will, sir. I will . . . I certainly will.

The Beggar leaves the stage in the direction from which he entered

Peachum (*ingratiatingly to the audience*) Gentlefolk all, in the hope of your gracious approval, we present *The Beggar's Opera* . . . Play away the Overture!

During the following air, the actors move according to the director's choreography

	Air 2: Through All The Employments of Life
Peachum	Thro' all the employments of life,
	Each neighbour abuses his brother;
	The making of money means strife
	As we rob and we plunder each other.
Men	So why blame the bold highwaymen?
Women	Please pity your sister, the whore;
All	For we're all after higher pay when
	We do it for more and for more.
Peachum	The lawyer demands his fat fee,
Women	It's certainly fatter than mine.
Peachum	And the priest counts his stipend while he
Men	Tells his beads at his office divine.
Peachum	For these are the rules of the game:
	There's no-one does nothing for nought.
	In high life and low it's the same:
Men	You loot and you rob——
Women	Or you're bought.
Peachum	Whatever your station, my dears,

Men	Should you work with your hands
Women	Or your brain.
Peachum	Be like statesmen or prelates or peers.
	Just be sure that your watchword is gain.
Men	For a man must be proud of his labour
	And industry must be his guide,
Peachum	So grab all you can from your neighbour
All	As you ride and you ride and you ride.
Women	Yes, we ride and we ride and we ride.
Men	Oh, we ride and we ride and we ride
All	For we ride and we ride and we ride,
	Ah, we ride and we ride and we ride.

All but Mr and Mrs Peachum leave, R *and* L

The rest of the stage is illuminated

ACT I

SCENE 1

The Peachums' house

The room is furnished with a desk and chair. The desk holds a large ledger, an ink bottle and a quill pen. There is also a couch and an occasional table. Mr and Mrs Peachum have remained on stage after the Prologue

Peachum (*to the audience*) I have at my command a gang of highwaymen. My business is to dispose of the goods they steal. In short, I am a fence . . . a suspect profession. But so that my business might flourish, I have to keep in with the law. Hence, I am also an informer. In practice, it all works admirably, for, if one of my highwaymen proves to be drunken, deceitful or lazy, I inform against him and receive the forty pounds reward for his hanging. Be they dead or alive, I make my profit. (*He sits at the desk*) Now, my dear, let's study the register of my gang.

Mrs Peachum (*glancing over his shoulder*) Looking for an execution against the next sessions, are you?

Peachum Ah, well, the Justices do so rely upon me, you know. (*He turns the pages of the ledger and studies them*) Now, let's see, who shall we deliver up? Harry Paddington? Ben Budge, Jemmy Twitcher, Matt of the Mint? Who shall we recommend for the noose this time?

Mrs Peachum Anyone you choose, my dear, as long as it isn't Captain Macheath.

Peachum rises and moves to C, *turning towards her, beaming with satisfaction*

Peachum Captain Macheath! Ah, now, there's a highwayman, to be sure. Makes me a fortune. I'll never deliver him up. He's the wealthiest gentleman on the road.

Mrs Peachum Oh, good. I'm pleased about that on Polly's account.

Peachum Polly's account? (*To the audience*) What the plague does the woman mean? Polly's account?

Mrs Peachum Captain Macheath is very fond of Polly.

Peachum Our daughter? (*Aroused*) My dearest partner, what are you saying? You are not suggesting that our Polly should marry him?

Mrs Peachum But if Polly's in love, how can we help it?

Peachum (*impatiently*) Lookee, m'dear, lookee! We must keep 'em apart! Should those two marry, it'll be our undoing.

Mrs Peachum Undoing?

Peachum Absolute ruin!

Mrs Peachum Eh?

Peachum (*moving around the stage*) Beloved, have you no discretion?

Married to Macheath . . . *never*! (*Thumping the ledger*) Polly knows
how we make our money. She knows of every transaction I have writ
down. If she marries Macheath, how can we be safe? We'll be in her
husband's power. For a husband has absolute authority over all a wife's
secrets. Besides, my daughter to me should be like the mistress of a
Prime Minister: a key to the whole gang. (*He calls*) Filch! Married?
Never! If the affair is not already done, I'll terrify her from it. Filch!
(*Yelling*) Filch!

Filch the Peachums' servant enters L

Filch Sir?
Peachum Where's my daughter?
Filch In t'other room, sir.
Peachum I'll to her straight. I'll sift the baggage. Married? Never!

Peachum leaves L

Mrs Peachum Come hither, Filch. (*She puts an arm round him and says
to the audience*) I am as fond of this child as though he was my own.
He hath as fine a hand at picking a pocket as a woman. (*To Filch*) If an
unlucky session doth not cut the rope of thy life, I pronounce, boy, thou
wilt be a great man in history. (*She pats him on the back and walks a
few steps from him*) Hark you, my lad, do you know what hath passed
between Captain Macheath and our Polly? And don't tell me a lie, for
you know how I hate a liar.
Filch I beg you, madam, don't ask me, for I must either lie to you or
Miss Polly—and I promised her I would not tell.
Mrs Peachum But Filch, what's the value of a promise worth when the
honour of the family is concerned? (*She takes his hand*) Come, Filch,
come with me into my own room. I'll give thee a most delicious glass of
that cordial that I keep for my own drinking.

Mrs Peachum and Filch leave R

Peachum and Polly enter L. *He drags her by an arm*

Peachum Are you married, you slut? Tell me, are you married or no?
Polly Father, hear me speak.
Peachum (*releasing her*) Well?
Polly (*moving* DR) Trust my discretion, please, Papa. I know as well as
any of the fine ladies how to make the most of myself. A woman knows
how to be mercenary, though she hath never been at court or at an
assembly. We have it in our natures, Papa. If I allow Captain Macheath
some trifling liberties, I have this watch (*indicating a fob watch, pendant
and bracelet*) and other visible marks of his favour to show for it. A
girl who cannot grant some things, and refuse what is most material,
will make but a poor hand of her beauty, and soon be thrown upon the
common.

Polly moves C. *Peachum moves* DL

Air 3: Virgins Are Like the Fair Flower

Virgins are like the fair flow'r in its lustre,
Which in the garden enamels the ground.
Near it the bees in play flutter and cluster,
And gaudy butterflies frolic around.
But, when once pluck'd, 'tis no longer alluring,
To Covent Garden 'tis sent, as yet sweet.
There fades, and shrinks, and grows past all enduring,
Rots, stinks, and dies, and is trod underfeet.

Peachum (*approaching Polly reassuringly*) You know, Polly, I am not against your toying and trifling with a customer in the way of business, or to wheedle a secret or so. (*Threateningly*) But if I find out that you have played the fool and are married, you jade, you, I'll cut your throat, hussy. Now you mind!

Mrs Peachum enters R. *She rushes across stage to* DL

Mrs Peachum (*with great passion*) A-a-a-ah!

Air 4: Our Polly is A Sad Slut

Our Polly is a sad slut! Nor heeds what we have
    taught her.
I wonder any man alive will ever rear a daughter!
For she must have both hoods and gowns and hoops
    to swell her pride,
With scarves and stays and gloves and lace; and
    she will have men beside!

Mrs Peachum chases Polly round the stage, ending with Polly backing to R

You baggage! You hussy! You inconsiderate jade! Had you been hanged it would not have vexed me, but to do such a mad thing by choice!

Peachum Wife! Wife, what is it?

Mrs Peachum (*joining Peachum*) The wench is married, husband. Married!

Peachum Married?

Mrs Peachum Married! I've just dragged it from Filch. She's married.

Peachum (*moving to Polly*) Polly, Polly, what have you done? Do you think your mother and I should have lived comfortably so long together, if ever we had been married?

Mrs Peachum You baggage! To think of it, my sweet bed-fellow, after all the advice we've given her from her tenderest years up!

Air 5: Can Love Be Controlled By Advice?

Polly (*moving to centre*)

Can love be controlled by advice?
Will Cupid our mothers obey?
Tho' my heart were as frozen as ice,
At his flame 'twould have melted away.
When he kissed me so closely he pressed,

'Twas so sweet that I must have complied.
So I thought it both safest and best
To marry, for fear you should chide.

(*She falls on her knees with clasped hands held out to her Parents*) But I did not marry him for honour or money as 'tis the fashion, but because I love him.

Mrs Peachum Love him! Worse and worse! I thought the girl had been better bred. (*To her husband*) Oh, my dearest dear, her folly makes me mad! My head swims! I'm distracted! I can't support myself—— Oh! (*She staggers about the stage and collapses on to the couch, as if fainting*)

Peachum See, wench, to what a condition you have reduced your poor mother! A glass of cordial, this instant!

Polly exits R

How the poor woman takes it to heart!

Polly returns quickly, pouring cordial from a bottle into a glass. She gives the bottle and glass to Peachum

Ah, hussy, this is the only comfort your poor mother has left! Sup it up quickly, my dear.

Polly Give her another glass, sir; my mamma drinks double the quantity whenever she is out of sorts. This, you see, revives her.

Mrs Peachum The child shows so much concern, that I could almost find it in my heart to forgive her. (*She rises*)

Air 6: O Polly, You Might Have Toy'd

Mrs Peachum   O Polly, you might have toy'd and kiss'd.
By keeping men off, you keep them on.
Polly   But he so teas'd me,
And he so pleas'd me,
What I did, you must have done.

Mrs Peachum But not with a highwayman, you sorry slut!

Peachum (*taking Mrs Peachum aside to the desk and turning the pages of the ledger*) A word with you, Missus. I have a thought shall soon set all matters to right. Were we not looking for an execution against the next sessions?

Mrs Peachum We were. Yes, we were.

Peachum Then leave her to me. (*He moves to Polly*) Why so melancholy, Polly? Since what is done cannot be undone, we must all of us endeavour to make the best of it. Sit!

Polly sits on the couch

So, Polly, you are married to Macheath, it seems? (*He joins Polly on the couch*)

Polly Yes, sir.

Peachum And tell me, Polly, have you not the common view of a gentlewoman in your marriage? Of a hope of becoming a widow?

Polly A widow?

Peachum But that, surely, is the whole scheme and intention of marriage articles. The comfortable state of widowhood is the only hope that keeps up a wife's spirits. Where is the woman who would scruple to be a wife, if she had it in her power to be a widow whenever she pleased? If you have any views of this sort, Polly, I shall think the match not so very unreasonable.

Polly How I dread to hear your advice! Yet I must beg you to explain yourself.

Peachum Secure all possessions he hath got, then have him 'peached at the next sessions . . .

Polly (*rising*) 'Peached?

Peachum Yes. Inform against him, hand him over to the gallows, and then at once you are made a rich widow.

Polly What . . . murder the man I love? The blood runs cold in my heart with the very thought of it!

Peachum (*rising*) Fie, Polly! What hath murder to do with the affair? The thing must happen sooner or later. I daresay the Captain himself would prefer we should get the reward for his death rather than a stranger.

Mrs Peachum Your duty to your parents, hussy, obliges you to hang him. What would many a wife give for such an opportunity!

Air 7: Oh Ponder Well

Polly   Oh, ponder well! Be not severe;
             So save a wretched wife!
             For on the rope that hangs my dear
             Depends poor Polly's life.

Should you make me a widow, I know my heart, I cannot survive him!

Air 8: The Turtle Thus

             The turtle thus with plaintive crying,
             Her lover dying,
             The turtle thus with plaintive crying,
             Laments her dove.
             Down she droops, quite spent with sighing,
             Pair'd in death, as pair'd in love.

Peachum and Mrs Peachum come down on either side of her

Thus, sir, it will happen to your poor Polly . . . the end.

Mrs Peachum What, is the fool in love in earnest, then? I hate thee for being so particular. Why, wench, thou art a shame to thy very sex.

Polly But hear me, Mother. If you have ever loved——

Mrs Peachum Those cursed play-books she reads have been her ruin. One word more, hussy, and I shall knock your brains out, if you have any.

Peachum (*threateningly*) Hence out of my way, Polly, for fear of mischief, and think on what I have proposed to you.

Mrs Peachum Away, hussy. Hang your husband and be dutiful to your loving parents.

Polly leaves L *but listens outside*

Peachum (*holding his wife's hands*) It all falls out nicely, my dear.

Mrs Peachum I'm not contradicting. Only our Polly might find it very hard when she sees the rope round his neck.

Peachum Yes, poor lamb.

Mrs Peachum I'll undertake to manage our Polly . . . give her what comfort I can in her sad bereavement.

Peachum (*returning to his ledger*) Thank ye. And I'll inform against Captain Macheath. Here I have it all writ down. I charge Macheath with highway robbery . . . the magistrates write a warrant . . . the Constables arrest him . . . and he is tried and hanged at the next session . . . for a price, mark you, for a price.

Air 2 (reprise): Through All the Employments of Life

Peachum	Of all the employments of life,
	To kill one's own kind is sad.
	I then must make sure that the price
	I receive for his death is not bad.
Mrs Peachum	It will break his old heart, I confess,
	For what man likes killing his friends?
	I'll make sure that they pay in excess,
	For money alone makes amends.
Mr and Mrs Peachum	Yes, money alone makes amends.

Peachum and Mrs Peachum exit R

Polly enters L

Polly Now I am a wretch indeed! My parents would have him hanged . . . and they'll do it! Methinks I see him already in the cart, sweeter and more lovely than the nosegay in his hand! I hear the crowd extolling his resolution and intrepidity. I already see him at the tree! The whole circle are in tears—even butchers weep! Jack Ketch himself hesitates to perform his duty, and would be glad to lose his fee by a reprieve.

Air 9: My Heart Forbodes

My heart forbodes he will die and be hung,
Tho' how can I believe it?
I see him pale and cold with death
As Tyburn now he nears it.
Beneath his left ear they fit a cord
The noose encircling his life is.
The youth in the cart hath the air of a lord,
And I will cry, 'There goes my Adonis'.

What, then, will become of Polly? But where is my beloved now? On

the heath? Would he were here at my side that I might warn him of
their design. Oh, my husband, what danger surrounds you! Should
their plot succeed—and you make that journey to Tyburn—then I
cannot survive you. . . . (*She sobs, her head resting on an arm of the
couch*)

*Then we hear an unaccompanied voice, quietly at first, but increasing in
volume to full-throated masculinity*

As Polly becomes aware of the voice, she leaps up in delight

Macheath (*off*) **Air 10: My Heart Was So Free**
La-la-la-la-la
La-la-la-la-la
La-la-la-la-la-la-la-la-la-
La-la-la-la-la——

Macheath enters R

Polly (*running to him*) My Captain!
Macheath (*holding her hands*) My Polly!
My heart was so free,
It roved like the bee
Till Polly my passion requited.
I sipped each flower
I changed ev'ry hour
But now ev'ry flower is united.
I sipped each flower,
I changed ev'ry hour
But now ev'ry flower is united.

They embrace

Polly My husband!
Macheath My wife!

Air 11: Pretty Polly Say
Pretty Polly, say,
When I was away,
Did your fancy never stray
To some newer lover?
Polly Without disguise,
Heaving sighs,
Doting eyes,
My constant heart discover.
(*Her head on his shoulder*)
Fondly let me loll!
Fondly let me loll!
Macheath O pretty, pretty Poll!
Polly Do you love me as ever, my dear?

Macheath Suspect my honour, my courage, suspect anything but my love. May my pistols misfire and my mare slip her shoulder while I am pursued, if I ever forsake thee! To tear me from thee is impossible.

They sing the following air with hands clasped or holding each other tenderly

Air 12: Were I Laid On Greenland's Coast
Were I laid on Greenland's coast
And in my arms embraced my lass:
Warm amidst eternal frost
Too soon the half year's night would pass.

Polly   Were I sold on Indian soil,
Soon as the burning day was clos'd
I could mock the sultry toil
When on my charmer's breast repos'd.

Macheath   I would love you all the day,
Polly   Every night would kiss and play,
Macheath   If with me you'd fondly stray
Polly   Over the hills and far away.

Air 12 can be repeated at the director's discretion

Polly Yes, I would go with thee. But oh! how shall I speak of it? I must be torn from thee. (*Clutching him more tightly*) We must part.
Macheath How! Part?
Polly We must, we must! (*Pushing him from her*) My papa and mamma are set against thy life. They now, even now are in search after thee. They would inform against thee and have thee hanged.
Macheath But why?
Polly They know we are married. Were you dead, I should be a wealthy widow and they would partake of the spoils. Part we must.

Air 13: Oh What Pain It Is To Part
Polly (*holding Macheath to her*)
Oh, what pain it is to part!
Can I leave thee, can I leave thee?
Oh, what pain it is to part!
Can thy Polly ever leave thee?
But lest death my love should thwart,
And bring thee to the fatal cart,
(*Pushing him away*)
Thus I tear thee from my bleeding heart!
Fly hence, and let me leave thee.

(*They kiss*) One kiss and then—(*they kiss again*)—begone—farewell!
Macheath My hand, my heart, my dear, is so riveted to thine, that I cannot unloose my hold.
Polly But my papa might intercept thee, and then I should lose the very glimmering of hope. A few weeks, perhaps, may reconcile us all. Shall thy Polly hear from thee?

Macheath If you doubt it, let me stay—and be hanged.

Polly Oh, how I fear! How I tremble! Go—but when safety will give thee leave, you will be sure to see me again; for till then, Polly is wretched indeed.

They embrace

Macheath Farewell!
Polly Farewell!

They part, looking back at each other with fondness. Macheath leaves R, *Polly, sobbing quietly, leaves* L

The Lights dim

SCENE 2

A Tavern

The furniture of Scene 1 is exchanged by the Highwaymen for a table, RC, *which has on it wine, brandy, tankards, pipes and tobacco. There are also a few stools and chairs. Present are Jemmy Twitcher, Crook-Fingered Jack, Wat Dreary, Robin of Bagshot, Nimming Ned, Henry Paddington, Matt of the Mint, Ben Budge and other members of the gang, as the director desires*

During the spell of dimness the Musicians play the tune of "Fill Ev'ry Glass". When the lights come up again, the Highwaymen have formed a tableau round the table. One of them has one foot on a stool and the other on the table

Air 14: Fill Ev'ry Glass

Highwaymen   Fill ev'ry glass, for wine inspires us
                                And fires us
                                With courage, love and joy.
                                Women and wine should life employ;
                                Is there aught else on earth desirous?
                                Fill ev'ry glass, for wine inspires us
                                And fires us
                                With courage, love and joy.

Jem bangs down his tankard, wipes his lips with the back of his hand

Jem Tell me, dear comrades and highwaymen all . . . tell me this: why are the laws levelled against us? Are we more dishonest than the rest of mankind? What we win, gentlemen, is ours by the law of arms and the right of conquest.

Ned You speak true! Furthermore, who is there here that would not die for his friend?

Harry Who is there here who would betray him for his interest?

Matt Show me a gang of politicians who can say as much.

Ben We are for a just partition of this world, for every man hath a right to enjoy life.

Matt Where is the injury, then, of taking from another what he hath not the heart to make of use of?
Robin And who are the true robbers of mankind?
Ned The rich.
Jem The miserly.
Ben The covetous.
Crook Those with an unused superfluity.
Others Well said!
Jem Fill the tankards!

They fill their tankards and sing again

Highwaymen   Fill ev'ry glass, for here the truth is:
                    Our youth is
                    Brutish, dicing with death.
                    Yet, 'ere the hangman takes our breath,
                    Women and wine shall make the noose bliss.
                    Fill ev'ry glass, for here the truth is:
                    Our youth is
                    Brutish, dicing with death.

Macheath enters L

Macheath Gentlemen, well met!

He moves to C. *Those not already standing leap to their feet*

All (*roaring*) Macheath! . . . The Captain! . . . Macheath! Hooray!
Macheath Gentlemen! Gentlemen! No ceremony, I beg you!
Matt We await you, Captain. There is e'en now a coach upon the Western Road full of rich travellers.
Macheath Your pardon, Matt. I cannot lead you this night.
Ben Not lead us?
Macheath I stand in some difference with Peachum. He would inform against me and have me hanged.
Jem Inform against you . . . never!
Wat I'd shoot him through the head first.

There is a general murmur of agreement

Macheath Peace, Wat! Peace, Jem! Peace, all of you! Peachum is a receiver and a necessary agent to us. The moment we break loose from him, our gang is ruined.
Matt What would you, Macheath?
Macheath I would have Peachum believe that I have quit the gang.
All Quit the gang?
Macheath Which I can never do but with life. Trust me, I prithee, and get about your business.
Matt Aye, Captain, aye. We are your servants and shall ever obey your instructions in all things. (*To the others*) Let us repair to our several duties, gentlemen.

Air 15: Let Us Take the Road

All   Let us take the road.
Hark! I hear the sound of coaches!
The hour of attack approaches,
To your arms, brave boys, and load.
See the guns we hold!
Let chemists toil like asses,
Our fire their fire surpasses,
And turns all our lead to gold.

All leave, except Macheath

Macheath Married I am ... married! But denied my wife's bed. Peachum has seen to that. What am I to do? Fidelity? Huh! A man might as well be contented with one guinea as with one woman! Singleness of affection has never been my way. No ...

Air 16: If The Heart Of A Man

If the heart of a man is depress'd with cares,
The mist is dispell'd when a woman appears;
Like the notes of a fiddle, she sweetly, sweetly,
Raises the spirits and charms our ears.
Roses and lilies her cheeks disclose,
But her ripe lips are more sweet than those.
Press her, caress her,
With blisses, her kisses
Dissolve us in pleasure and soft repose.
Press her, caress her,
With blisses, her kisses
Dissolve us in pleasure and sweet repose.

(*Calling loudly*) Drawer! Drawer!

The Drawer of the Tavern enters R

Is the porter gone search for the choicest ladies in town according to my instructions?

Drawer I expect him back every minute with the very cream of the bawdy-houses from Vinegar Lane to Hockley-in-the-Hole.

The bar bell jangles

That's the bar bell. Sure, some of them are below.

Macheath Then show them up!

Drawer Indeed I will, sir, straight.

Drawer leaves R

Macheath I must have women. There is nothing unbends the mind like them. Money is nothing near so strong a cordial as the entwined limbs of a woman.

Drawer ushers in R *the Ladies of the Town—Mrs Coaxer, Dolly Trull,*

Mrs Vixen, Betty Doxy, Jenny Diver, Mrs Slammekin, Suky Tawdry and Molly Brazen

Welcome, ladies, welcome!

To the background of the Air, "Youth's The Season Made For Joys", Macheath greets each lady in turn

Dear Mrs Coaxer, you are welcome. You look charmingly today. I hope you don't want the repairs of quality, and lay on paint. Dolly Trull! Kiss me, you slut; are you as amorous as ever, hussy? Ah, Dolly, thou wilt ever be a coquette. Mrs Vixen, I'm yours. I always loved a woman of wit and spirit; they make charming mistresses, but plaguey wives. Betty Doxy! Come hither, hussy! Do you drink as hard as ever? You had better stick to good wholesome beer; for in troth, Betty, strong waters will ruin your constitution. What! And my pretty Jenny Diver, too! As prim and demure as ever! Mrs Slammekin! Always so careless and genteel. But see, here's Suky Tawdry and Molly Brazen!

Molly kisses him

That's well done. I love a free-hearted wench. Come, ladies, sing me that French tune Mrs Slammekin was so fond of.
Slammekin *Youth's The Season*, do you mean?
Macheath That's the one.

	Air 17: Youth's The Season
Chorus of	Youth's the season made for joys,
Ladies	Love is then our duty.
	She alone who that employs
	Well deserves her beauty.
	Let's be gay,
	While we may,
	Beauty's a flower, despis'd in decay.
	Youth's the season made for joys,
	Love is then our duty.

     Let us drink and sport today,
Ours is not tomorrow.
Love with youth flies swift away,
Age is nought but sorrow.
Dance and sing,
Time's on the wing,
Life never knows the return of spring.
Let us drink and sport today,
Ours is not tomorrow.

Some Ladies sit, some take wine. Macheath takes up a position between Jenny and Mrs Coaxer

Macheath Drawer, bring us more wine!

The Drawer exits R

If any of the ladies choose gin, I hope they will be so free to call for it.

Jenny You look as if you meant me. Wine is strong enough for me. Indeed, sir, I never drink strong waters, but when I have the colic.

Coaxer Why, you'd never find our Jenny drunk. She must keep her wits about her. No woman has a greater art in the picking of her lover's pocket than our dear Jenny . . . and she does it as coolly as if money were her only pleasure. Don't you, Jenny?

Jenny I never go to the tavern with a man but in the view of business. I have other sorts of men for my pleasure.

Trull (*moving to the side of Mrs Coaxer and addressing Jenny*) But pray, madam, weren't you ever in keeping?

Jenny I hope, madam, I han't been so long upon the town, but I have met with some good fortune as well as my neighbours.

Trull Pardon me, madam, I meant no harm by the question; 'twas only in the way of conversation.

Jenny Indeed, madam, if I had not been such a fool, I might have lived very handsomely with my last friend. But upon his missing five guineas, he turned me off.

Slammekin Tut-tut . . . shame!

Jenny I never suspected he counted them.

Slammekin You were tempted and took . . . I know, love, I know.

Jenny (*to Macheath*) But to be sure, sir, with so much good fortune as you have had upon the road, you must be grown immensely rich.

Macheath The road, indeed, hath done me justice, but the gambling table hath been my ruin.

Jenny (*taking one of the two pistols in his belt*) This is the tool of a man of honour. Cards and dice are only fit for cowardly cheats, who prey upon their friends.

Tawdry (*taking Macheath's other pistol*) This, sir, is fitter for your hand. Besides your loss of money, 'tis a loss to the ladies. Gambling takes you off from women. How fond could I be of you! But before company 'tis ill-bred.

Macheath Wanton hussies! I must and will have a kiss to give my wine a zest. Come, kiss me, Jenny.

Jenny 'Tis not convenient, sir, to show my fondness among so many rivals. 'Tis your own choice, but not the warmth of my inclination that will determine you.

During Air 18 Jenny ties a blindfold over Macheath's eyes and everyone begins to play Blind Man's Buff

Air 18: Before the Barn Door
Before the barn door crowing,
The cock by hens attended,
His eyes around him throwing,

Stands for a while suspended.
Then one he singles from the crew,
And cheers the happy hen;
And how d'you do, and how d'you do,
And how d'you do again.

Chorus of   Before the barn door crowing,
Ladies   The cock by hens attended,
His eyes around him throwing,
Stands for a while suspended.
Then one he singles from the crew,
And cheers the happy hen;
And how d'you do, and how d'you do
And how d'you do again.

The song builds to a great crescendo while Macheath plays Blind Man's Buff with the Ladies

Peachum and two Constables enter R

Macheath "catches" Peachum

Peachum I seize you, sir, as my prisoner.
Macheath Peachum! (*He snatches off his blindfold*)

The Constables grab Macheath's arms

Who has done this to me? Beasts, jades, jilts, harpies, furies, whores! Who has done this?

Peachum throws Jenny a purse of money

Was this well done, Jenny?
Peachum Your case, Mr Macheath is not particular. The greatest heroes have been ruined by women. And, to do them justice, I must own they are very pretty creatures, if we could trust them. The gentleman, ladies, lodges in Newgate. Constables, conduct the Captain to his lodgings.

Air 19: At The Tree I Shall Suffer
Macheath   At the tree I shall suffer with pleasure,
At the tree I shall suffer with pleasure.
Let me go where I will,
In all kinds of ill,
I shall find no such furies as these are.
Let me go where I will,
In all kinds of ill,
I shall find no such furies as these are.

Macheath leaves R, *guarded by the two Constables and Peachum*

Jenny We shall go aside and share out the spoils. But first let us celebrate our trade with a song.

Air 17 (reprise): **Youth's The Season**

Ladies   Youth's the season made for joys,
              Love is then our duty.
              She whose body well employs
              Shall receive the booty.
              Let's be gay,
              While we may,
              Beauty's a flower despis'd in decay.
              Youth's the season made for joys,
              Love is then our duty.

The Ladies leave, with Jenny waving aloft the purse of money
The lights dim, the furniture is removed and the scene changes

SCENE 3

Newgate Prison

The prison is indicated by three frames of wooden laths painted black which represent iron bars. The frames are situated L, R *and* UC. *They leave gaps for entrances and exits at* DL, UL, DR *and* UR. *A table and stool are set on stage*

On one frame are hooks and pegs from which dangle a variety of hand-cuffs

Lockit, Macheath and the Constables enter R

Lockit Noble Captain, you are welcome. You have not been a lodger of mine this year and a half. You know the custom, sir. Garnish, Captain, garnish. (*To a Constable*) Hand me down those fetters there.

The Constable obeys

Macheath Those, Mr Lockit, seem to be the heaviest of the whole set. (*indicating a different pair*) With your leave, I should like the further pair better.

Lockit Look ye, Captain, we know what is fittest for our prisoners. When a gentleman uses me with civility, I always do the best I can to please him. We have them of all prices, from one guinea to ten, and 'tis fitting every gentleman should please himself.

Macheath I understand you, sir.

Macheath gives Lockit money

Lockit Methought you would. (*To the Constable*) Take down the further pair.

The Constable does so. These particular fetters are of gleaming light-weight brass with a long chain connecting the two cuffs

Do but examine them, sir . . . never was better work. How genteely they are made! They will fit as easy as a glove, and the nicest man in England might not be ashamed to wear them. (*He puts the chains on Macheath*) And so, sir . . . I now leave you with your private meditations.

Lockit and the Constables leave L

Macheath (*striding backwards and forwards down stage*) Meditations!

Air 20: Man May Escape
Man may escape from rope and gun;
Nay, some have outliv'd the doctor's pill;
Who takes a woman must be undone,
That basilisk is sure to kill.
The fly that sips treacle is lost in the sweets,
So he that tastes woman, woman, woman,
He that tastes woman ruin meets.

He sits on stool R

To what a woeful plight have I brought myself! Here must I be confined all day long till I am hanged to hear the reproaches of a wench who lays her ruin at my door. I have promised marriage to Lockit's daughter, Lucy. The moment she knows I am here, a fine time between this and my execution I shall have.

Lucy (*off*) Captain Macheath! Captain Macheath!

Macheath Here she comes! Would that I were dead!

Lucy enters L. *She is clearly pregnant*

Lucy You base man, you! How can you look me in the face after what hath passed between us? See here, (*indicating her swelling stomach*) perifidious wretch, how I am forced to bear about the load of infamy you have laid upon me. Oh, Macheath! Thou hast robbed me of my quiet . . . to see thee tortured would give me pleasure.

Macheath Have you no bowels, no tenderness, my dear Lucy, to see a husband in these circumstances?

Lucy What do you mean . . . husband?

Macheath Well, husband in everything but name, and that, my dear Lucy, can be arranged at any time. But lovers should not insist upon ceremonies. From a man of honour, his word is as good as his bond.

Lucy All you fine men take pleasure in insulting the women you have ruined, don't you?

Air 21: How Cruel Are The Traitors
How cruel are the traitors,
Who lie and swear in jest,
To cheat unguarded creatures
Of virtue, fame and rest!
Whoever steals a shilling,
Through shame the guilt conceals;
In love the perjured villain
With boasts the theft reveals.

Macheath (*moving to her*) Have patience! The very first opportunity, my dear, you shall be my wife in whatever manner you please.

Lucy (*shaking her fist in his face*) Insinuating monster! And so you think I know nothing of your affair with Miss Polly Peachum. Oh, I could tear your eyes out! (*Her nails approach his eyes, so he grasps her wrists*)

Macheath Sure, Lucy, you can't be such a fool as to be jealous of Polly!

Lucy Are you not married to her, you brute, you?

Macheath Married to her? Huh! (*He moves* L) The wench gives it out only to vex thee, and to ruin me in thy good opinion. Indeed, my dear Lucy, these violent passions may be of ill consequence to a woman in your condition ...

Lucy (*following him*) Come, come, Captain, for all your assurance, you know that Miss Polly hath put it out of your power to do me the justice you promised me.

Macheath To convince you of my sincerity, if we can find the Chaplain, I shall have no scruples of making you my wife ... and I know the consequence of having two at a time.

Lucy That you are only to be hanged, and so get rid of them both.

Macheath (*taking her hand in mock sentiment*) I am ready, my dear Lucy, to give you satisfaction, if you think there is any in marriage. What can a man of honour say more?

Lucy So then, it seems, you are not married to Miss Polly.

Macheath You know, Lucy, the girl is prodigiously conceited. No man can say a civil thing to her but, like other fine ladies, her vanity makes her think he's her own for ever and ever. (*He moves to* C, *occasionally addressing some of the lines of the following Air to Lucy*)

Air 22: The First Time At The Looking-Glass
The first time at the looking-glass
The mother sets her daughter,
The image strikes the smiling lass
With self-love ever after.
Each time she looks she, fonder grown,
Thinks ev'ry charm grows stronger.
But alas, vain maid, all eyes but your own
Can see you are not younger.

When women consider their own beauties, they are all alike unreasonable in their demands; for they expect their lovers should like them as long as they like themselves.

Lucy (*indicating off*) Yonder is my father. Come! This way we might light upon the Chaplain who shall try if you will be as good as your word. For I long to be made an honest woman! Come! Quickly ... come!

Lucy and Macheath leave UR

Enter Peachum and Lockit UL. *Lockit carries an account book. They move to* C

Lockit In this latest affair, brother Peachum, we are agreed. You have consented to go halves in the reward money for Macheath.

Peachum We shall never fall out about an execution. But as to that article, pray how stands our last year's account?

Lockit If you will run your eye over it, you'll find 'tis fair and clearly stated. (*He gives the book to Peachum who studies it*)

Peachum These long arrears of the government are very hard on us. Tut, tut, tut, unless people in authority can pay better for their hanging, I promise them for the future, I shall let other rogues live beside themselves.

Lockit Yes, we are treated by them with contempt, as if our profession were not reputable.

Peachum In one respect, indeed, our employment may be considered dishonest, because, like great politicians, we encourage those who betray their friends.

Lockit Shh! Such language, brother! Learn to be more guarded, I beg you.

Air 23: When You Censure The Age

When you censure the age,
Be cautious and sage
Since authority offended could be.
If you mention vice or bribe,
'Tis so pat to all the tribe
Each cries, "That was levelled at me."

Peachum Whatever man's estate,
You will find him profligate,
So be careful who it is you do defame.
Call your serving-wench a whore
And the lady from next door
Will cry, "Sir, did you mention my name?"

Lockit When vice is so rife, 'tis a pity on my life
Should you ever try to cleanse this world of sin.
Tell the bishop in his see you're opposed to sodomy.
And he'll think you are talking of him.

Peachum Ask any magistrate
Why his knowledge is so great
In the catalogue of theft and vice and crime,
He'll not think of it as praise for his legalistic ways,
But suspect you know he's at it all the time.

Lockit People in a lowly way
Must be careful what they say,
For libel's only worth while if you're rich.
There's a parliamentary man
Who will slander all he can
And then hide behind the rules of privilege.

**Lockit
and
Peachum** When we have a loyal friend
Upon whom we can depend,
A friendship that's been well and truly tried,
Beware the hasty slip

That could break our partnership
And leave us both a-dangling side by side.

Lucy enters L

Peachum sits at the table R, *studying Lockit's account book*

Lockit Whence come you, hussy?

Lucy I have been looking for the Chaplain, Father, for I have much to confess. (*She joins her father*)

Lockit Confess? And so I should think. You have been whimpering and fondling, like a spaniel, over the fellow that hath abused you.

Lucy One can't help love; one can't cure it. 'Tis not in my power to obey you, and hate him.

Lockit Let him be your husband and then have him die, like any reasonable woman. No woman would ever marry if she had not the chance of mortality for a release. Act like a woman of spirit, hussy, and thank your father for what he is doing.

Air 24: Is Then His Fate Decreed, Sir?

Lucy
Is then his fate decreed, sir?
Such a man can I think of quitting?
When first we met, so moves me yet,
Oh, see how my heart is splitting.
Oh! See how my heart is splitting!

Lockit Look ye, Lucy, there is no saving him. So, I think, you must even do like other widows—buy yourself weeds and be cheerful.

Air 25: You'll Think Ere Many Days

You'll think, ere many days ensue,
This sentence not severe;
I hang your husband, child, 'tis true,
But with him hang your care.
Twang dang dillo dee.
Derry derry I doh, a doh, I doh
Derry derry I doh, a doh dee.

Like a good wife, go moan over your dying husband. That, child, is your duty. Consider, girl, you can't have the man and the money too. So make yourself easy of mind by getting all you can from him.

Lucy leaves UL, *sobbing and moaning*

Peachum (*rising and approaching Lockit*) Here's poor Ned Clincher's name, I see. Surely, brother Lockit, it was a little unfair proceeding against Ned. He told me in the condemn'd hold that for the money he gave you, you had promised him a session or two longer without molestation.

Lockit Mr Peachum, this is the first time my honour was ever called in question. He that attacks my honour, attacks my livelihood. And this usage, sir, is not to be borne.

Peachum Since you provoke me to speak, I must tell you, too, that Mrs Coaxer charges you with defrauding her of the information money for the apprehending of Curl-pated Hugh. Indeed, indeed, brother, we must pay our spies punctually, or we shall have no information.

Lockit Is this language to me, sirrah—who has saved you from the gallows, sirrah?

They seize hold of each other's collar

Peachum If I am hanged, it shall be for ridding the world of an arrant rascal.

Lockit This hand shall do the office of the halter you deserve, and throttle you, you dog!

Peachum Brother, brother, we are both in the wrong. We shall both be losers in the dispute, for you know we have it in our power to hang each other! You should not be so passionate. (*He releases his grasp on Lockit*)

Lockit Nor you so provoking. (*He releases his grasp on Peachum*)

Peachum If I said anything, brother, to the prejudice of your character, I ask pardon.

Lockit I can forgive as well as resent. Give me your hand.

They shake hands

Peachum Brother Lockit.
Lockit Brother Peachum.

Air 23 (reprise)

Peachum	When we have a loyal friend
and	On whom we can depend,
Lockit	A friendship that's been well and truly tried,
	Beware the hasty slip
	That could break our partnership
	And leave us both a-dangling side by side.

Peachum and Lockit leave UR *with their arms round one another's shoulders*

the CURTAIN *falls*

ACT II

Scene 1

Newgate Prison

The setting is as before, with the addition, at extreme DL, *or apron, of a wooden armchair. This will represent Lockit's room as the scene progresses. This area also contains a clothes stand on which the Chaplain's broad-brimmed black hat and gown are hanging*

Macheath and Lucy enter UL

Lucy Though the Chaplain was not to be found today, I hope, my dear, you will upon the first opportunity quieten my scruples.

Macheath Oh, I shall, my dear, I shall. Now to my escape.

Lucy Oh, sir, my father's hard heart is not to be softened.

Macheath But if I could raise a small sum—would not twenty guineas, think you, move him? Of all the arguments in the way of business, the bribe is the most prevailing. Your father's perquisites for the escape of prisoners must amount to a considerable sum in the year. Money well timed and properly applied will do anything.

Lucy What love or money can do shall be done; for all my comfort depends upon your safety.

Polly enters L

Polly Where is my dear husband? (*She rushes to Macheath*) Was a rope ever intended for this neck? Oh, let me throw my arms about it, and throttle thee with love.

Macheath turns and walks away from her

What means my love? Why dost thou turn away from me? 'Tis thy Polly—'tis thy wife!

Macheath Was ever such an unfortunate rascal as I am!

Lucy Was there ever such another villain!

Polly runs to him and twists him round by the shoulder

Polly Oh, Macheath! Was it for this we parted? Taken? Imprisoned! Tried! Hanged! Cruel reflection! I'll stay with thee till death. No force shall tear thy dear wife from thee now.

Macheath turns away

What means my love? Not one kind word? Not one kind look? Think what thy Polly suffers to see thee in this condition.

Macheath (*aside*) I must disown her. The wench is distracted.

Lucy rushes to him and twists him round by the shoulder

Lucy Am I then cheated of my virtue? Can I have no reparation? Sure, men were born to lie, and women to believe them. O villain! Villain!

Macheath moves to c

Polly Am I not thy wife? Thy neglect of me, thy aversion to me, too severely proves it. (*She rushes to Macheath*) Look on me! Tell me, am I not thy wife?

Lucy (*running to Macheath*) Perfidious wretch!

Polly Barbarous husband!

Lucy Had thou been hanged five months ago, I had been happy.

Polly And I, too. If you had been kind to me till death, it would not have vexed me—and that's no very unreasonable request to a man who hath not above seven or eight days to live.

Lucy Art thou then married to another?

Macheath If women's tongues can cease for an answer—hear me.

Lucy I won't! Flesh and blood can't bear my usage.

Polly Shall I not claim my own? Justice bids me speak.

Air 26: How Happy Could I Be With Either

Macheath   How happy could I be with either,
Were t'other dear charmer away!
But while you thus tease me together,
To neither a word will I say!
But tol de rol tol de rol laddy,
And tol de rol tol de rol lay,
But tol de rol tol de rol laddy,
And tol de rol tol de rol day!
But tol de rol tol de rol laddy,
And tol de rol tol de rol lay,
But tol de rol tol de rol laddy,
And tol de rol tol de rol day!

Polly (*moving to his side*) Sure, my dear, there ought to be some preference shown to a wife. You must be distracted with your own misfortunes, or you could not use me thus.

Lucy (*moving to his other side*) O villain, villain! Thou hast deceived me. I could even inform against thee with pleasure. I must have satisfaction!

Air 27: I'm Bubbled

Polly   I'm bubbled,
Lucy   I'm bubbled.
Polly   Oh, how I'm troubled!
Lucy   Bamboozled and bit!
Polly   My distresses are doubled.
Lucy   When you come to the tree, should the hangman refuse,
These fingers, with pleasure, could fasten the noose.
Polly   I'm bubbled,

Lucy	I'm bubbled,
Polly	Oh, how I'm troubled!
Lucy	Bamboozled and bit!
Polly	My distresses are doubled.
Lucy	When you come to the tree, should the hangman refuse,
	These fingers, with pleasure, could fasten the noose.

Macheath (*leading Lucy* L) Be pacified, my dear Lucy—this is all a trick of Polly's to make me desperate with you in case I get off. If I am hanged, she would fain have the credit of being thought my widow. (*He leads Polly* R) Really, Polly, this is no time for a dispute of this sort; for whenever you are talking of marriage, I am thinking of hanging.

Polly And hast thou the heart to persist in disowning me?

Macheath And hast thou the heart to persist in persuading me that I am married? Why, Polly, dost thou seek to aggravate my misfortunes?

Lucy (*moving to the couple*) Really, Miss Peachum, you do but expose yourself. Besides, 'tis barbarous in you to worry a gentleman in his circumstances.

Polly

Air 28: Cease Your Funning
Cease your funning,
Force or cunning!
Never shall my heart trepan.
All these sallies
Are but malice
To seduce my constant man.

'Tis most certain,
By their flirting,
Women oft have envy shown:
Pleas'd to ruin
Others' wooing;
Never happy in their own!

Decency, madam, methinks, might teach you to behave yourself with some reserve towards the husband, while his wife is present.

Macheath But seriously, Polly, this is carrying the joke a little too far.

Lucy (*moving to Polly*) If you are determined, Madam, to raise a disturbance in the prison, I shall be obliged to send for the turnkey to show you the door. I am sorry, Madam, you force me to be so ill-bred.

Polly Give me leave to tell you, Madam, that these forward airs don't become you in the least, Madam. And my duty, Madam, obliges me to stay with my husband, Madam.

Macheath moves R, *sits and buries his head in his hands*

During the following Air, Lockit has the opportunity to enter DL *and move unobtrusively to his chair, where he falls into drunken slumbers*

Air 29: Why, How Now, Madam Flirt?

Lucy Why, how now, Madam Flirt?
If you thus must chatter,
And are for flinging dirt
And are for flinging dirt,
Let's try who best can spatter,
Madam Flirt!

Polly (*to Lucy*) Why, how now, saucy jade!
For sure the wench is tipsy!
(*to Macheath*) How can you see me made,
How can you see me made
The scoff of such a gypsy?
(*to Lucy*) Saucy jade!

Macheath (*rising*) Why, how now, ladies fair,
I beg you cease this slanging.
An error has been made somewhere,
An error has been made somewhere,
But my mind's on my hanging!
Ladies fair!

Polly Why, how now, rampant ram,
and Lucy We're fearful for your life.
Lucy I'll save thee from the tree if I can;
Polly I'll save thee from the tree if I can!
Polly But who's your lawful wife?
and Lucy Rampant ram!
Lucy Why, how now, wanton whore,
I have his child within me,
And so demand by common law,
And so demand by common law,
My husband that he shall be!
Wanton whore!

Polly Why, how now, sweet mistress!
I fear this fact might hurt you,
But marriage lines I do possess,
But marriage lines I do possess,
Dear lass of easy virtue,
Sweet mistress!

Peachum enters, UL

Peachum Where's my wench? Ah, hussy, hussy! (*He approaches Polly*) Come you home, you slut; and when your fellow is hanged, hang yourself, to make your family some amends.

Polly Dear, dear Father, do not tear me from him. I must speak! I have more to say to him. (*She runs to Macheath* R) Oh, twist thy fetters about me, that he may not haul me from thee!

Polly ducks her head under the chain of his fetters, whilst Lucy moves to his L *and takes his arm*

Peachum Sure, all women are alike! If ever they commit the folly, they are bound to commit another by exposing themselves. Easy—not a word more—you are my prisoner now, hussy.

Air 30: No Power On Earth

Polly   No power on earth can e'er divide
                 The knot that sacred love hath tied
                 When parents draw against our mind,
                 The true-love's knot they faster bind.
                 Ho Ho rah in amborah
                 Ho an ho derry hi am hi derry Hoo
                 Hoo derry derry derry derry am borah.

There now ensues a tug-o'-war. Lucy tugs at Macheath's arm, but his fetters are about Polly's neck, whilst Peachum is pulling Polly's arm. The struggle seems impossible until Macheath ducks his head and Polly is released, only to be dragged off-stage UL *by Peachum*

Macheath I am naturally compassionate, Lucy, so that I could not use the wench as she deserved; which made you at first suspect there was something in what she said.
Lucy Indeed, my dear, I was strangely puzzled.
Macheath Lucy, my sweet, make me, if possible, love thee more. I prithee, procure my escape, I beg you.
Lucy My father, I know, hath been drinking with the prisoners and, I fancy, he is now taking a nap in his own room. If I can, I shall procure the keys.
Macheath Good lass—let's seal it with a kiss. (*He kisses her*) Obtain the keys and my heart is thy prisoner forever.
Lucy I shall do it deftly, for the Chaplain's gown lies also in his room. Anything for your escape, gratitude and love.

Lucy walks on tip-toe to DL *of the stage which represents Lockit's room*

Lockit starts to snore. He holds his heavy bunch of keys on his lap. Lucy creeps behind him and makes a buzzing sound of a fly

Lucy Z-z-z-z-z . . .

She touches with a finger his left cheek. Lockit imagines a fly has alighted on him. Without opening his eyes, he lets go of the keys and tries to knock the fly off his face. Lucy snatches the keys, the Chaplain's gown and broad-brimmed black hat. She then creeps quietly back to Macheath, unlocks his handcuffs and helps him into the Chaplain's gown

Lucy Let me dress thee (*she giggles*)—whilst my heart would undress thee. Shall I go off with thee, my dear, in thy escape?
Macheath If we are together, 'twill be impossible to lie concealed. Our bodies will be entwined in love—and that would delay matters. No. As soon as the search begins to be a little cool, I will send for thee. Till then, my mind, spirit and desires shall ever rest thy captive.

Lucy Go, then, my dear Captain . . . owe thy life to me . . . and be grateful.

Macheath A moment of time may make us unhappy forever.

They embrace briefly and Macheath leaves UR

Lockit gradually awakens

Lockit The keys! The keys! Who's took 'em? (*He rises and moves to Lucy*) Lucy! Lucy! Where is he? Where's Macheath? (*He shouts*) Jailers! Ring the alarum! Clang the escape bell! Find me my fugitive— or be hanged, the lot of you!

There is a loud clanging of a bell and a tumult from other prisoners, off

Lucy, Lucy! (*Threatening*) To be sure, wench, you must have been aiding and abetting to help him slip my fingers.

Lucy No blame can lie with me, sir. Here hath been Peachum and his daughter, Polly. And to be sure, they know the ways of Newgate as well as if they had been born and bred in the place. Why should your suspicions light on me?

Lockit Lucy, dear Lucy! None of these shuffling answers. Did he tip you handsomely, eh? How much did he pay you? Come, hussy, don't cheat your honest father and I shall not be angry with you. Perhaps you have made a better bargain with him than I could have done. How much gold did he give you, my good girl?

Lucy As you suspect, sir, I am fond of him and would have given of our own money to have kept him with me.

Lockit (*horrified*) Oh, Lucy! Our own money? Thy education, my dear, might have put thee more upon thy guard.

Lucy My education!

Lockit Even a girl in the bar of an ale house receives a little extra for good services.

Lucy Speak not of my education or of my lowering myself to be a barmaid. For 'tis to your instruction I owe my ruin.

Air 31: When Young At The Bar
When young, at the bar, you first taught me to pour
And bid me be free with my lips and no more;
I was kissed by the parson, the squire and the sot;
When the guest was departed, the kiss was forgot.
But his kiss was so sweet, and so closely he pressed,
That I languished and pined till I granted the rest.

Lockit (*grabbing and shaking her*) And so you have let him escape, hussy, have you? (*He releases her*)

Lucy When a woman loves, a kind look a tender word can persuade her to anything—and I could ask no other bribe.

Lockit (*amazed*) No other bribe? Oh, will you never learn the ways of business?

Lucy tosses her head, turns her back and walks UR

Thou wilt always be a vulgar slut, Lucy.

Lucy (*turning*) But love, sir, is a misfortune that may happen to the most discreet woman, and in love we are all fools alike.

Lockit So you mean to marry him, eh?

Lucy No, sir. Notwithstanding all he swore, I am fully convinced that Polly Peachum is truly his wife. Did I let him escape, fool that I was, to go to her? Polly will wheedle herself into his money, and then Peachum will hang him, and cheat us both.

Lockit (*moving to Lucy*) So I am to be ruined, because, forsooth, you must be in love! A very pretty excuse!

Lucy I could murder Polly Peachum, that impudent, happy strumpet! I gave him his life and that creature enjoys the fruits of it. Ungrateful Macheath! (*She moves to* C)

Air 32: My Love Is All Madness and Folly

My love is all madness and folly,
Alone I lie,
Toss, tumble and cry!
What a happy creature is Polly!
Was e'er such a wretch as I!
With rage I redden like scarlet,
That my dear inconstant varlet,
Stark blind to my charms,
Is lost in the arms
Of that jilt, that inveigling harlot!
Stark blind to my charms,
Is lost in the arms
Of that jilt, that inveigling harlot!
This, this my resentment alarms.

Lockit And so, after all this mischief, I must stay here to be entertained with your caterwauling, Mistress Puss! Out of my sight, wanton strumpet! (*He waves to* UL *exit*) You shall fast and mortify yourself into reason with, now and then, a little handsome discipline, to bring you to your senses. Go!

Lucy leaves UL

Lockit addresses the audience whilst prowling about the stage

Peachum then intends to outwit me in this affair; but I'll be even with him. The dog is leaky in his liquor, so I'll ply him that way, get the secret from him, and turn this affair to my own advantage. Lions, wolves and vultures don't live together in herds, droves or flocks. Of all animals of prey, man is the only sociable one. Every one of us preys upon his neighbour, and yet we herd together. Peachum, my companion, my friend, may quote thousands of precedents for cheating me. Shall I not make use of the privilege of friendship to make him a return?

Air 33: Thus Gamesters United
Thus gamesters united in friendship are found,
Though they know that their industry all is a cheat;
They flock to their prey at the dice-box's sound,
And join to promote one another's deceit.
But if by mishap
They fail of a chap,
To keep in their hands, they each other entrap.
Like fish lean with hunger, who miss of their bait,
They bite their companions and feed on their mate.

(*Shouting*) Lucy!

Lucy enters UL

Are there any of Peachum's people now in the house?

Lucy Filch, sir, is in the next room, at the service of Black Moll.

Lockit Bid him come to me.

Lucy leaves UL

(*To the audience*) Now then, Peachum, you and I, like honest tradesmen, are to have a fair trial which of us can outdo the other.

Filch enters UL. *He is lean, stumbling and pallid. He approaches Lockit*

Why, boy, thou lookest as if thou wert half-starved, like a shotten herring.

Filch Oh, sir, one needs have the constitution of a horse to go through this business. Since the favourite child-getter was disabled by over-working of himself, I have picked up a little money by helping the ladies to a pregnancy against their being hanged. But if a man cannot get an honest livelihood an easier way . . .

Lockit Boy, canst thou tell me where thy master can be found.

Filch At his warehouse, sir, near the sign of The Crooked Billet.

Lockit Thank you, lad. Very well, then we'll go see Peachum. Macheath shall not remain a day longer out of my clutches.

Lockit and Filch move off UL

The lights dim. Prison scenery, furniture and props are rapidly removed

SCENE 2

A highway

An open stage. Night. The Highwaymen enter DL *singing disconsolately their earlier song*

Air 14 (reprise)
Highwaymen   So we took the road
                     But have heard no sound of coaches.

              No chance of attack approaches.
              Unload, brave boys, unload.
              We have had no luck.
              Without Macheath to lead us,
              There is no gold to pluck.

Macheath enters, UR, *still dressed as the Chaplain. He spreads his arms with a gun in one hand and his broad-brimmed black hat in the other. His voluminous gown flies open and reveals his normal clothes*

Macheath Gentlemen, well met!
Highwaymen (*joyously*) Macheath! Macheath!

Macheath takes C *stage with the Highwaymen grouped round him*

Macheath I'm sorry, gentlemen, the road was so barren of money. When my friends are in difficulties, I am always glad that my fortune can be serviceable to them. (*He gives them money*) You see, gentlemen, I am not a mere Court friend, who promises everything and will do nothing.

Air 34: The Modes of the Court

              The modes of the Court so common are grown,
              That a true friend can hardly be met;
              Friendship for interest is but a loan,
              Which they let out for what they can get.
              'Tis true, you find,
              Some friends so kind,
              Who'll give you good counsel themselves to defend.
              In sorrowful ditty,
              They promise, they pity,
              But shift you for money from friend to friend.

Macheath   'Tis true, you find,
and   Some friends so kind,
Highwaymen Who'll give you some counsel themselves to defend.
              In sorrowful ditty,
              They promise, they pity,
              But shift you for money from friend to friend.

Macheath But we, gentlemen, have still honour enough to break through the corruptions of the moneyed tyrants in their coffee houses. And while I serve you, you may command me.
Highwaymen Hooray for Macheath! Hooray!
Macheath   The modes of the Court, as all of you know,
              Have but one maxim: self-interest.
              Turn but a coin, your friend becomes foe,
              When money's involved, then count us your guest.
              'Tis true there are those
              Who'll make you suppose
              That they will supply you with money you lack.
              They drink your good health
              But once you've no wealth

	Then daggers are drawn for a stab in the back.
Macheath	'Tis true there are those
and	Who'll make you suppose
Highwaymen	That they will supply you with money you lack.
	They drink your good health
	But once you've no wealth
	Then daggers are drawn for a stab in the back.

The voices of Lockit and Filch are heard off R

Lockit (*off*) So this is the way to Peachum's warehouse where he keeps his vast hoard of stolen goods?

Filch (*off*) It is indeed so, Mr Lockit.

Highwaymen (*in hushed voices*) Lockit . . . Lockit . . . It's Mr Lockit!

Macheath Then a funeral, lads, a funeral! We've done it before in stopping a coach.

Rapidly a Highwayman leaps on to the shoulders of the others. They hold him as if he were a stiff corpse. Macheath follows behind, as a Chaplain, hands holding an open prayer book, head bowed

(*chanting*) "The Lord is my shepherd; I shall not want. He maketh me to lie down in green pastures; He leadeth me beside the still waters . . ."

Lockit and Filch enter R, *carrying lanterns*

They remove their hats and place them over their hearts in reverence, whilst bowing their heads in respect as the "funeral procession" passes

Filch (*gesturing* L) Onwards, Mr Lockit, onwards! 'Tis this way Peachum's hide-out is to be found.

The "funeral procession" moves off R

Filch and Lockit go off L

The lights dim

SCENE 3

Peachum's Warehouse

Peachum and a Servant are examining a chest of loot C. *There is a table* L *with wine, liquors and glasses. There is a rack of clothes* UR, *two chairs near the table and another small table near the chest*

Peachum Damask cloth, gold thread . . . Holland sheets, rich brocade . . . snuff boxes, silver plate . . . (*He jots the items down in his ledger*)

There is a heavy knock on the door. Peachum and the Servant freeze and listen. Another knock

Peachum Go spy who it is.

The Servant leaves R

(*To the audience*) It cannot be the law, for the law is in my pocket.

The Servant returns R

Servant It's Mr Lockit.
Peachum Lockit! Go let him in. (*He nods at the Servant*)

The Servant exits

Lockit enters R

Lockit Where is he, then? Where is the Captain?
Peachum Captain?
Lockit Captain Macheath, brother!
Peachum Captain Macheath! I trust he is in Newgate, brother!
Lockit No, brother, he has escaped. (*He draws his sword*) Hand him over if he is beneath this roof.
Peachum Are you accusing me of sheltering a man whose neck's so well-fitted for the noose? (*He draws a longer sword*)
Lockit (*retreating in a placatory manner*) Oh, no, no, brother, you are much mistook. Would you not agree, brother, that our daughters are two slippery hussies?
Peachum My Polly is one, for sure.
Lockit Then I beg you, brother, keep a watchful eye on your Polly, as I shall upon my Lucy. For Macheath sniffs after the pair of them and so, in a day or two, the prisoner shall be our own again.

The Servant enters R

Servant Sir, sir, there's a woman outside who would speak with you.
Peachum What woman?
Servant She's the woman that keeps the brothel, sir.
Peachum Brothel?
Servant Yeah, brothel.
Peachum What brothel? Speak more clearly, man. You talk as if the town had only one.
Servant I stand corrected, sir. It is Mrs Diana Trapes.
Peachum Dye Trapes, eh? Shall we admit her, brother Lockit?
Lockit By all means. She's a fine-spoken woman . . . a woman who drinks so freely and blabs so heartily, that none of her customers' secrets is safe.
Peachum (*pouring liquor into a glass for Lockit*) Desire her to walk in.

The Servant exits

You're right, brother. A wondrous source of information to us is Mrs Dye.

Mrs Trapes enters. During the scene she drinks freely of Peachum's liquor

Peachum Mrs Dye, your servant. (*He sweeps her an elegant bow*)
Mrs Trapes My dear Mr Peachum. (*She kisses him*)
Peachum One may know by your kiss that your gin is excellent.

Mrs Trapes I was always very curious in my liquors Mr Lockit! (*She kisses him also*)

Lockit There is not a perfumed breath like it! I have long been acquainted with the flavour of those lips, haven't I, Mrs Dye?

Mrs Trapes I take as large a draught of liquor as I did of love. And I hate a flincher in either!

During the following Air, Mrs Trapes occasionally dances a few sprightly steps, sometimes involving momentarily Peachum and Lockit as her partners

Air 35: In the Days of My Youth

Mrs Trapes In the days of my youth I could bill like a dove,
Fal lal lal lal lal lal re riddle addy.
Like a sparrow at all times was ready for love
Fal de riddle addy,
Fal de riddle addy,
Fal lal lal lal lal lal la la laddy.

The life of all mortals in kissing should pass,
Fal lal lal lal lal lal re riddle addy.
Lip to lip while we're young, then the lip to the glass.
Fal de riddle addy,
Fal de riddle addy,
Fal lal lal lal lal lal la la laddy.

All The drink I imbibed put my mind in despair,
Fal lal lal lal lal lal re riddle addy,
Mrs Trapes I remember the day when my face was still fair.
All Fal de riddle addy,
Fal de riddle addy,
Fal lal lal lal lal lal la la laddy.

Mrs Trapes I yearn and I burn as the more I do sip,
All Fal lal lal lal lal lal re riddle addy,
Mrs Trapes Not for lip to the glass but for lip to the lip.
All Fal de riddle addy,
Fal de riddle addy
Fal lal lal lal lal lal la la laddy.

Mrs Trapes collapses, spread-eagled in the chair

Mrs Trapes Oh, if only I could again be bedded by a handsome young man, I'd give up a bottle or two any old day. (*She rises and moves to the table to take a swig from a bottle*) Now, Mr Peachum, to business. What stolen goods have you that I might sell to my ladies? (*Noticing a pendant*) Ooh! What's your lowest price for this? (*She picks up the jewelled pendant from the table*)

Peachum (*taking it from her*) Now look you, Mrs Dye, you deal so hard with me that I can ill afford to give the gentlemen who venture to steal these goods little or nothing.

Mrs Trapes 'Tis hard times, I know, 'tis hard times. 'Tis the fault of the government. Our parliament is making great cuts upon us in the way of business.

Peachum You speak truth, Mrs Dye. Left to the politicians, there'll very soon be hardly a man of private, honest trade left in the land!

Mrs Trapes We run great risks, great risks indeed. Five of my sweetest girls are now laid low with the pox. What with the surgeon's fees and other expenses, there are great goings-out and no comings-in.

Peachum We are wrapt round with tragedy, Mrs Dye. We solitary souls, employed only by our own selves, giving our all to further the common-wealth, are wrapt round with tragedy.

Mrs Trapes (*crossing to* DR, *swigging from a bottle*) There's a way, Mr Peachum, there's a way.

Lockit There is?

Mrs Trapes (*turning*) Certainly there is. (*She moves* UR) I'll not buy clothes for any girl of mine, the taxes being what they are under this government. No! I leaves 'em naked.

Peachum Naked?

Mrs Trapes (*moving between Peachum and Lockit*) Let their customers buy them clothing if they please—but customers don't, do they?

Peachum Not those given to natural delights, no.

Mrs Trapes Agreed. Consider that sweet, riggish, juicy, aching-for-the-fray, dear soul I have, Mrs Coaxer.

Lockit Ah, my dear Mrs Coaxer. . . .

Mrs Trapes Two hours ago, I stripped her of her clothing, and left her waiting, as she ought to be, naked for the Captain.

Lockit (*alert*) The Captain?

Mrs Trapes If the Captain should need for his delights a petticoat and bodice to ruffle and then tear asunder, let him pay for them, that's what I say.

Lockit The Captain? What Captain?

Mrs Trapes Why, Captain Macheath, to be sure.

Peachum⎫
⎬Captain Macheath?⎰ (*Speaking together*)
Lockit⎭

Lockit Where is he?

Mrs Trapes (*with tipsy dignity*) He is performing a private transaction with Mrs Coaxer. Afore business commences, he likes to see her prettily dressed.

Peachum With Mrs Coaxer, you say?

Mrs Trapes He is with her now.

Peachum Come, Lockit!

Lockit Come, Peachum!

Peachum Let's make haste.

Peachum and Lockit leave R

Mrs Trapes (*moving to clothes rack*) I shall take some of these widows' weeds with me to sell to my girls. For the dear souls have great sensibilities and upon their clients' hanging, always wish to be seen dressed in black at the gallows. God bless 'em.

She selects black garments from the clothes rack. She staggers to the chest and removes some silver plate, and then to the table from which she takes a bottle of liquor. She swigs from it as she leaves, R

The lights dim

SCENE 4

Newgate Prison

When the lights come up again, the set has been rearranged to what we have seen before at Newgate Prison, with the omission of Lockit's chair and the clothes stand. There is now a silver salver with cordial and two glasses set on the table R

Lucy is alone, C

Lucy Jealousy, rage, love and fear are at once tearing me to pieces. Now I am weather-beaten and shattered with distresses!

Air 36: I'm Like A Skiff
I'm like a skiff on the ocean toss'd,
Now high, now low, with each billow borne,
With her rudder broke and her anchor lost,
Deserted and all forlorn.
While thus I lie rolling and tossing all night,
That Polly lies sporting on seas of delight!
Revenge, revenge, revenge,
Shall appease my restless sprite!
While thus I lie rolling and tossing all night,
That Polly lies sporting on seas of delight!
Revenge, revenge, revenge,
Shall appease my restless sprite.

Polly has sent word that she would come visit me. Why, I know not. But I have not been idle. I have some rats' bane here. (*She produces a small phial from the bosom of her dress and pours it into one of the glasses on the table* R) Ready to poison her with. I run no risk, I can lay her death upon the gin, and so many die of that naturally these days that I shall never be called in question. (*Slightly fearfully*) But say I were to be hanged? (*Confidently*) I never could be hanged for anything that would give me greater comfort than the poisoning of that slut!

Filch enters UL

Filch Madam, here's Mistress Polly come to wait upon you.
Lucy Show her in.

Filch shows in Polly UL, *then he exits*

Miss Peachum, your servant. (*She bobs a curtsy*)

Polly (*bobbing a curtsy*) Miss Lockit, your servant.

Lucy I hope you will pardon my passion when I saw you last, but I was so overrun with the spleen, that I was perfectly out of myself. And really, when one has the spleen, everything is to be excused by a friend.

Polly I, too, must claim your pardon for my own behaviour, madam. It is for this reason I am come.

Lucy I admire your civility, Miss Polly. And in the way of friendship, will you give me leave to propose a glass of cordial to you? (*She moves to the table*)

Polly I hope, madam, you will excuse me, but strong waters are apt to give me the headache.

Lucy Headache? Never! (*She pours the cordial into the two glasses*) I assure you, Polly, one taste of my liquor and you'll have perfect peace. (*She offers Polly the poisoned glass of cordial*) Come, Polly, let us drink.

Polly (*shaking her head*) I am sorry, madam, my health will not allow me to accept strong waters.

Lucy But what ails you, Polly?

Polly The Captain has treated me with so much contempt and cruelty, madam.

Lucy Tell me, have you seen him since his escape?

Polly (*wailing*) No!

Lucy Then our cases, my dear Polly, are exactly alike. Both of us have been too fond and are now deserted. Indeed, my dear Polly, we are both of us a cup too low. Let me prevail upon you to accept of my offer. I can't bear, child, to see you in such low spirits. And I must persuade you to what I know will do you good.

Polly accepts the poisoned glass

(*Aside*) I shall soon be even with the hypocritical strumpet.

Polly (*aside*) All this wheedling of Lucy's cannot be for nothing. By pouring strong waters down my throat, she thinks to pump some secrets out of me. I'll be on my guard, and won't taste a drop of her liquor, I'm resolved.

Air 37: Come, Sweet Lass

Lucy

> Come, sweet lass,
> Let's banish sorrow
> Till tomorrow;
> Come, sweet lass,
> Let's take a chirping glass.
> Wine can clear
> The vapours of despair
> And make us light as air.
> Then drink and banish care.
> Come, sweet lass,

Polly	I'll not drink it,
	Never think it.
Lucy	Come, sweet lass,
	And take a chirping glass.
Polly	Joy is such
	That I must dance and trip (*she starts to dance*)
	But e'er I take a sip,
	The glass falls from my lip.

Polly drops the glass

Oh, how clumsy of me! Pray pardon me, I'm all of a dither.

From UL *Macheath enters in heavy hand-cuffs and chains. He is accompained by Peachum, Lockit and two Constables*

They move across the stage in slow march time to Macheath's table where he sits. A Constable removes the salver with its bottle and glasses

The Constable exits DR

Ah, what do I see? Macheath again in custody!

Lucy and Polly rush to him

Lucy (*holding him closely to her from behind his chair or stool*) My lover!
Polly (*kneeling at his feet and clasping his hands*) My husband!
Lockit Set your hearts at rest. The Captain has neither the chance of love or money for another escape. He is ordered to be called down upon his trial immediately.
Peachum Away, hussies! This is not the time for a man to be hampered by his women.
Lucy Oh, husband, husband, my heart longed to see thee; but so see thee thus distracts me!
Polly Will my dear husband look upon his Polly? Why hadst thou not flown to me for protection? With me thou hadst been safe.

Air 38: Hither Dear Husband
Hither, dear husband, turn your eyes.

Lucy	Bestow one glance to cheer me.
Polly	Think, with that look, thy Polly dies.
Lucy	Oh, shun me not, but hear me.
Polly	'Tis Polly sues . . .
Lucy	'Tis Lucy speaks.
Polly	Is thus true love requited?
Lucy	My heart is bursting
Polly	. . . Mine, too, breaks.
Lucy	Must I
Polly	. . . Must I be slighted?

Macheath rises and moves to C

Macheath What would you have me say, ladies? You see this affair will soon be at an end, without my disobliging either of you.

Lucy and Polly follow him to C, *with imploring gestures*

Air 39: Which Way Shall I Turn Me?
Which way shall I turn me? How can I decide?
Wives, the day of our death, are as fond as a bride.
One wife is too much for most husbands to hear,
But two at a time there's no mortal can bear.
This way, and that way, and which way I will,
What would comfort the one, t'other wife would take ill.

Polly But if his own misfortunes have made him insensible to mine, a father, sure, will be more compassionate. Dear, dear sir . . . (*Polly kneels before Peachum* RC) sink the material evidence, and bring him off at his trial. Polly upon her knees begs it of you.

Lucy (*to Lockit,* LC) If Peachum's heart is hardened, sure you, sir, will have more compassion on a daughter. I know the evidence is in your power. How, then, can you be a tyrant to me? (*She kneels before her father*)

Lockit Macheath's time has come, Lucy. We know our own affairs, therefore cease your whimpering and whining.

Peachum Set your heart at rest, Polly. Your husband is to die today, therefore 'tis high time to look about you for another.

Polly bursts into protesting tears

Lockit We are ready, sir, to conduct you to the Old Bailey.

Air 40: The Charge Is Prepared
Macheath   The charge is prepared, the lawyers are met,
The judges all ranged, a terrible show.
I go undismayed, for death is a debt—
A debt on demand, so take what I owe.
Then farewell, my love—dear charmers, adieu!
Contented I die—'tis the better for you.
Here ends all dispute for the rest of our lives,
For this way, at once, I please all my wives.

Now, gentlemen, I am ready to attend you.

Macheath, held by a Constable, exits followed by Lockit and Peachum, who in turn are followed by Polly and Lucy. They all leave UR

The lights dim to out as we hear the Judge's sentence off. At the discretion of the director, a microphone, amplifier and loud-speakers could be useful here, making the Judge's words resound round the auditorium

Judge (*off*) Prisoner at the bar, the sentence of this court is that you shall be taken from this place, to a place hence, at Tyburn, there to be hanged by the neck until you are dead. And may the Lord have mercy upon your soul.

The lights come up again to their former level. Macheath re-enters UR *guarded by the Constables and followed by Lockit*

Lockit Garnish, Captain, garnish! Money is of no avail to you now, but I have something here that is. Allow me to make you a little more easy. (*He flourishes a bottle of brandy and a pewter mug which he puts on the table* DR) Unloose his fetters. He has no hope of escape this time. (*To Constables*) Come, let us secure all outer doors.

Macheath gives Lockit a bag of money

Lockit leaves UL, *followed by the Constables*

Macheath pours a large ration of brandy into the mug and drinks it. He will continue to do this during the rest of the scene

Air 41: O Cruel, Cruel Case

Macheath   O cruel, cruel case!
Must I suffer this disgrace?

Of all the friends in time of grief,
When threat'ning death looks grimmer,
Not one so sure can bring relief
As this best friend, a brimmer.

But can I leave my pretty hussies
Without one tear or tender sigh?
Their eyes, their lips, their busses,
Recall my love—ah, must I die?

He drinks deeply and wipes his mouth on his cuff

Since laws were made for ev'ry degree,
To curb vice in others, as well as me,
I wonder we han't better company
Upon Tyburn tree!
But gold from law can take out the sting,
And if rich men, like us, were to swing,
'Twould thin the land, such numbers to string
Upon Tyburn tree!

Enter a Constable UL

Constable Some friends of yours, Captain, desire to be admitted. I leave you together.

The Constable leaves UL

The Highwaymen enter UL

Matt We are heartily sorry, Captain, for your misfortune.
Macheath So am I, my friends, so am I . . . (*He shakes hands with them*) But gentlemen, look well to yourselves, won't you? For, in all probability, you may live some months longer.
Matt Aye, 'tis true. This is the place, gentlemen, where one day we must all of us come to.

Highwaymen (*murmur severally*) Aye . . . aye . . . 'tis here . . . e'en here
. . . no escape . . . fate decrees such . . . we know it.

Enter a Constable UL

Constable Miss Polly and Miss Lucy entreat a word with you.
Macheath Gentlemen . . . adieu.

He shakes hands with some and claps the shoulders of others

The Highwaymen leave UR

Polly and Lucy enter UL

Macheath (*as the girls approach him*) My dear Polly . . . my dear Lucy.
(*He swigs from the bottle*)
Polly How can I support this sight?
Lucy There is nothing moves one so much as a great man in distress.

Air 42: Would I Might Be Hanged
Would I might be hanged!

Polly	And I would so, too . . .
Lucy	To be hanged with you . . .
Polly	My dear, with you!
Macheath	Oh, leave me to thought! I fear! I doubt!
	I tremble, I droop . . . see my courage is out!

He upturns the empty bottle

Polly	No token of love?
Macheath	. . . see, my courage is out.

He upturns the empty mug

Lucy	No token of love?
Polly	Adieu!
Lucy	Farewell!
Polly	No token of love?
Lucy	Adieu!
Polly	Farewell!

The death-bell tolls

Macheath	But hark! I hear the toll of the bell!
Macheath, Polly	No token of love?
and Lucy	Farewell!
	No token of love
	Adieu!
	Farewell!
	But hark! I hear the toll of the bell,
	The toll of the bell,
	The toll of the bell.

The Constable enters UL

Constable Four women more, Captain, with a child apiece. See, here they come!

The Constable moves L

Four Women, carrying babies, enter

The Women surround Macheath

Women (*severally*) My husband . . . my spouse . . . father of our child . . . husband, dearest . . . my only man . . . husband . . . husband . . . husband . . .

Macheath What! Four wives more! This is too much!

He breaks through the group and moves to the Constable

Constable Have you a last request, sir?

Macheath Yes! Tell the sheriff's officers I am ready!

The lights dim

The prison grilles, stool and table are removed

The hangman's cart is pushed from the wings to UC, *so that the rear is presented to the audience. (If the hangman's cart is difficult to construct or there is not enough space in the wings to contain it, although it would be out of period, a stepped platform, representing a scaffold, can be placed* UC *instead.) Macheath leaps on to the cart and stands aloft. A noisy crowd gathers round the cart. The Women discard their prop babies in the wings, returning later to form part of the crowd*

A noose is lowered to a position behind Macheath's head

Jack Ketch is present in his black hood, together with the Highwaymen, Constables, Lockit, Peachum and other available male characters

The lights go up again

SCENE 5

Tyburn

Air 42 (reprise)

Macheath   All you who behold this terrible sight,
and Male   Consider your sins, for your souls are in plight.
Chorus   Captain Macheath sets example to you
                Whose hearts have forsaken the good and the true.
                Cut down in his prime of strength and youth,
                Who can but learn from so sad a truth?
                Cut down in his prime of strength and youth,
                Who can but learn from so sad a truth?

Macheath Allow me, gentlefolk, a final word. Since I must swing, I scorn to wince or whine. How am I come to this pass? 'Tis woman—my soul's luxury: woman. Tender and sweet of flesh, yet with hearts of vipers. I stand here for this: I have loved much; therefore I am betrayed much. So, farewell, life! Jack Ketch, do thy worst—for now I must die for kisses. That is . . . (*There is a pause. He raises his voice*) . . . unless the good citizens of London should wish to come to save me.

All available Women, including Polly and Lucy, dash on from R

Women A reprieve! A reprieve! We demand a reprieve!

Some carry placards on sticks with such slogans as "Save Macheath!", "Macheath shall not hang!", "Where Is Justice?", "Hands off Macheath!", "Peachum Go Home!", "Lock Lockit!"

Their cries resolve themselves into a rhythmical chant in which the Men also join

Crowd Mac-heath . . . *Re*-prieve . . . Mac-heath . . . *Re*prieve . . . Mac-heath . . . *Re*-prieve . . .

The Beggar rushes on from the L, *holding his battered script*

Beggar What's all this? Silence, will you? This is not my play! Quiet, all of you!

The crowd falls silent

You'll not alter a word of my play! And much damage have you done already!

Peachum What madness is this?

Beggar You'll not change my play. 'Tis my piece . . . writ from my heart and must be said exact!

Peachum (*aside*) A plague on all playwrights, say I. Now look here, sir —look here—

Beggar Why *you* . . . you whoreson rogue, thou hast changed my play and given it fresh conclusions. Macheath must be hanged! (*He bangs down his script*)

Peachum Calm, sir, calm. Come aside. In all things, we beggars must be pragmatical. Should we hang Macheath, the piece would have no happy ending.

Beggar A pox on your happy ending, say I! As I promised the spectators in my introduction, my piece shall be realistic.

Peachum "Realistic"! Oh, how terrible a word! Solely before the court do plays have any realism about them, and only then so that the rich nobility can shed their crocodile tears. If we were realistic, we'd have slit our own throats years ago. Dreams, brother, dreams are what we're made on.

Beggar But truth must surely out?

Peachum "What is truth?" said jesting Pilate and would not stay for an answer. Now come closer, sir. (*In his ear*) Are you not hypocritical?

Beggar Hypocritical? Me?

Peachum takes the Beggar by the arm and for the next few speeches they

stroll together across the front of the stage. The other "Actors" relax, awaiting the outcome

Peachum Did you not declare in your exposition that flattery will get you everywhere and honesty will get you nowhere?

Beggar I did, sir . . . Indeed I did.

Peachum And do we beggars not live by our wits? We are in no way political. Whatever the government, there are always jails. Our weighty task is to bamboozle and plunder wherever we can. Give the people a happy ending and the play will have excellent chances of being repeated.

Beggar "Repeated", you say?

Peachum For who wants tragedy when there is so much tragedy around us?

Beggar "Repeated" . . . hum-hum . . . I must think upon it . . . "Repeated"?

Peachum And with each fresh performance, you will be paid your dues.

Beggar Dues?

Peachum Money!

Beggar Money?

Crowd (*bellowing*) Money!

Peachum Money is hard to come by nowadays. There's hardly a purse along the common road worthy of the picking. What say you now, sir?

Beggar Well . . . er . . . taking all things into account, if a happy ending to all our present misfortunes is what the public wants—and what's more, if I am to receive much money into the bargain—why quibble? I therefore sacrifice my calvinistic conscience for the sake of the common weal. A happy ending it shall be! (*He throws his script into the air. The leaves scatter*)

Crowd Hooray! Hooray!

Beggar A happy ending forever, say I!

Peachum Come to my arms! At last you are a true and honest beggar. I congratulate you, sir.

Peachum and the Beggar embrace

The crowd cheers

Crowd Hurray! "Happy ending"! Hurray!

Peachum (*to the Beggar*) Thank you. Now withdraw, sir, and have faith.

The Beggar leaves

Company! Take it from "Macheath, Reprieve!" will you?

Crowd (*re-assembling*) Mac-heath . . . Re-prieve . . .

The Messenger rushes in from R *and kneels* C

Messenger I am a Messenger!

Peachum You are a Messenger?

Crowd He is a Messenger!

The Messenger rises

Messenger Hark ye! Hark ye! I am charged by His Most Glorious
   Britannic Majesty to deliver this, His Most Gracious Proclamation!
   (*He drops a scroll headed "Pardon"*) Macheath is pardoned!

The crowd gives a prolonged cheer

The Women dash to dispose of their placards in the wings and return

Crowd Hurray! Hurray! Hurray! . . .

Macheath leaps from the platform C

The noose rises and disappears

Macheath Pardoned? Ye gods, did he say "pardoned"?
Peachum You are pardoned.
Macheath (*leaping from the cart*) Dear sir, I thank you. How sweet it is to
   live—to be alive . . .

Macheath's women advance upon him

Women (*severally*) My love! My husband! Dear Captain! Beloved! Mine
   own! Your wife!
Macheath . . . or is it? Oh, ye gods, my wives!

Macheath is surrounded by his women

Women Ah, the Captain . . . my beloved . . . Captain! . . . Thou hast
   plighted thy troth to me! . . . My darling, come to thy wife in all but
   name! . . . He's mine! . . . He's promised! He's sworn!

Macheath dodges these women, only to be faced by Lucy

Lucy Noble Captain, come to my arms!
Macheath (*while wheeling round and escaping her*) Greetings, Lucy.

Macheath comes face to face with Polly, C

Polly Captain, I'm here! 'Tis your very own Polly!
Macheath Oh, heavens!
Polly I am thy true wife! I have the marriage articles, my darling. (*She
   produces them from the bosom of her dress, waves them in front of the
   other women and replaces them*)

The women quarrel, calling their lines almost together

Woman Marriage articles? No, never! He's promised to me.
Woman He's mine! Mine! He bed me first and would wed me later; he
   gave me his word.
Woman I've give him all; not only has he took my body, but he's took
   my heart with it.
Woman No woman has him but me. Marriage articles or no, I claim him.
Lucy This is a trick, Polly! Oh, that I had poisoned you! This is a trick!

Macheath leaps away from them on to the platform

Macbeth Ladies, ladies—sweet ladies! Look ye, all of you. Let us have

no controversy now. I am alive! I could be dangling from the gallows'
tree, but I am alive. And where's life, you have hope—so, my dears, let
us give this day to mirth—and I am sure she who thinks herself my
wife will testify her joy by a dance.

All Come, a dance . . . a dance!

Macheath (*to the men on stage*) Gentlemen, each of you take to his arms
a lady—and so dance.

*The men move to the ladies of their choice whilst Macheath leaps from the
platform to reach Polly*

Macheath Don't make others jealous, you sly slut!

Polly Slut!

Macheath (*taking her hands*) My dearest wife.

Polly My beloved husband!

Macheath Dance, shall we?

Polly Yes, my Captain—dance.

A simple dance is performed during the following Air

Air 43: Thus He Stands Like A Turk

Chorus   Thus he stands like a Turk with his doxies around,
From all sides their glances his passion confound,
For black, brown and fair, his inconstancy burns,
And the different beauties subdue him by turns.
Each calls forth her charms to provoke his desires,
Though willing to all, with but one he retires.
But think of this maxim and put off your sorrow:
The wretch of today may be happy tomorrow.
But think of this maxim and put off your sorrow:
The wretch of today may be happy tomorrow.

*All except Macheath and Polly continue singing this song whilst, still
dancing, they leave the stage, both* R *and* L

*All lights dim to out, except for the spot/s which illuminate Macheath and
Polly*

Once alone, Macheath embraces Polly

Air 12 (reprise)

Macheath	I will love you all the day,
Polly	And at night we'll kiss and play,
Macheath	And we'll roam at break of day
and Polly	Over the hills and faraway.
Macheath	O pretty, pretty Poll!

They embrace and kiss

The spot/s fade to out

As the actors take their calls and the company assembles for the final line-up, the director might wish to send the audience home happy by recalling one or a medley of some of the more boisterous tunes, sung by the entire company Perhaps the audience might join in too, even if their contribution is made by "la-las" and/or rhythmic hand claps

the CURTAIN *falls*

The director might decide to send the audience home during the recalling and of a number of scenes. The most obvious of these cuts is the end of Scene Re-hang the curtains behind Jenny in the Scene if there is sufficient room. If needed, they just make chair.

FURNITURE AND PROPERTY LIST

PROLOGUE

Bare stage

Personal: **Macheath:** brace of pistols
           Lockit: large bunch of heavy keys
           Highwaymen: single pistol in each belt

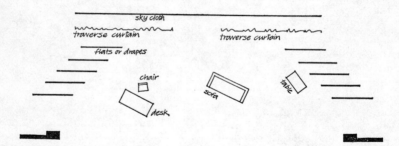

ACT I

SCENE 1

On stage: Desk. *On it:* ledger, quill pen, ink pot and sand castor
           Chair
           Couch
           Occasional table

Off stage: Bottle of cordial and glass **(Polly)**
Personal: **Polly:** Fob watch, pendant and bracelet
           Polly: Small handkerchief

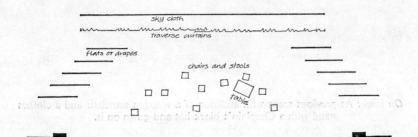

SCENE 2

Strike: Previous setting

Set: Table. *On it:* wine, brandy, tankards, pipes and tobacco
            Chairs
            Stools

Personal: **Jenny Diver:** Blind-fold
            Ladies: Fans and furbelows
            Peachum: Purse of money

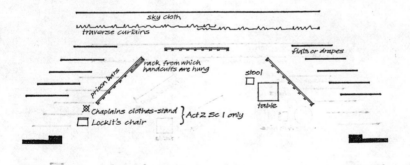

SCENE 3

Strike: Previous setting

Set: Frames L, UC and R
            On left frame: hand-cuffs of different weight and length of chain
            Table
            Stool

Off stage: Account Book **(Lockit and Peachum)**

Personal: **Macheath:** Bag of money

ACT II

SCENE 1

On stage: As previous scene with addition of a wooden armchair and a clothes stand with a Chaplain's black hat and gown on it.

Personal: **Lockit:** heavy bunch of keys

SCENE 2

Strike: Previous setting

Off stage: Prayer Book **(Macheath)**
Chaplain's hat and gown **(Macheath)**
Hats and lanterns **(Lockit and Filch)**

Personal: **Macheath:** money
Lockit: sword

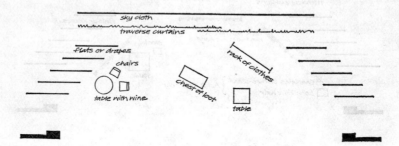

SCENE 3

Strike: Previous setting

On stage: Table. *On it:* wine, liquors, glasses
Two chairs

Chest. *In it:* damask cloth, gold thread, Holland sheets, rich brocade, snuff boxes, silver plate, watches on gold chains, pendant
Table
Rack of clothes, including widows' weeds

Personal: **Peachum:** sword

SCENE 4

Strike: Previous setting

Set: As in Act I, Scene 3

On stage: Table, *On it:* silver salver, cordial and glasses

Off stage: Brandy and pewter mug **(Lockit)**
Four property babies **(Ladies)**

Personal: **Lucy:** phial of rats bane
Macheath: heavy handcuffs and chains, bag of money

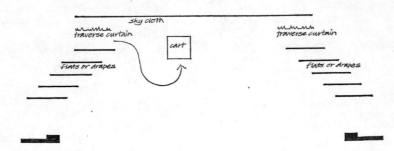

SCENE 5

Strike: Previous setting

On stage: Hangman's cart (or stepped platform) with noose above

Off stage: Placards on poles **(Ladies)**

Personal: **Jack Ketch:** hood
             Beggar: tattered script
             Messenger: scroll
             Polly: marriage articles

LIGHTING PLOT

Only essential cues are given. Other effects may be added at the Producer's discretion

Property fittings required: nil

Several interior and exterior settings: Peachum's house, a tavern, Newgate prison, a highway, Peachum's warehouse, Tyburn

Prologue

To open: Front of stage lit only

Cue 1   As all leave stage at end of Prologue   (Page 4)
           Lights up to full stage

ACT I, SCENE 1

Cue 2   At end of scene   (Page 13)
           Dim to half for scene change

ACT I, SCENE 2

To open: Full lighting

Cue 3   Ladies leave   (Page 19)
           Dim lights for scene change

ACT I, SCENE 3

To open: Prison lighting

No cues

ACT II, SCENE 1

To open: Prison lighting

Cue 4   **Lucy** tiptoes to **Lockit**   (Page 29)
           Spot on Lockit's "room"

Cue 5   **Lucy** creeps back to **Macheath**   (Page 29)
           Spot down on Lockit's "room"

Cue 6   **Lockit** gradually awakens   (Page 30)
           Slow fade up on Lockit

Cue 7   **Lockit** and **Filch** exit   (Page 32)
           Lights dim

ACT II, SCENE 2

To open: Moonlight

Cue 8   At end of scene   (Page 34)
           Dim lights for scene change

ACT II, Scene 3

To open: Interior lighting
Cue 9   At end of scene   (Page 38)
            Dim lights for scene change

ACT II, Scene 4

To open: Prison lighting

Cue 10   After general exit   (Page 41)
            Lights dim during Judge's speech then up to previous level

Cue 11   **Macheath: ". . . sheriff's officers I am ready".**   (Page 44)
            Lights dim

ACT II, Scene 5

To open: Tyburn, exterior lighting

Cue 12   All except Polly and Macheath exit   (Page 48)
            Lights dim to spot(s) on Macheath and Polly

Cue 13   **Macheath** (*singing*): ". . . pretty Poll"   (Page 48)
            Lights fade to black-out, then up to full for Finale

EFFECTS PLOT

Only essential cues are listed here. Further effects may be added at the Producer's discretion

ACT I

Cue 1 **Drawer: ". . . to Hockley-in-the-Hole"** (Page 15)
Bar bell jangles

ACT II

Cue 2 **Lockit: ". . . or be hanged the lot of you!"** (Page 30)
Bell clangs, prisoners shout

Cue 3 **Polly** (*singing*)**: "Farewell"** (Page 43)
Death bell tolls

MADE AND PRINTED IN GREAT BRITAIN BY
LATIMER TREND & COMPANY LTD PLYMOUTH
MADE IN ENGLAND